ALSO BY VERNA GILLIS

The I of the Storm
2020

Tales from Geriassic Park - On the Verge of Extinction
2019

I'll Never Know if I Would Have Gotten the Same Results If I'd been Nice: Terror Firma
2015

I Just Want to be Invited— I Promise Not To Come (life as one-liners)
2012

All titles available at amazon.com

AN INSIGHT JOB

AN INSIGHT JOB

VERNA GILLIS
THE OLDER

AN INSIGHT JOB

copyright © 2021 by Verna Gillis

Cover and book design by Elizabeth Cline

FIRST EDITION
ISBN-13: 978-0-578-30161-7

Grant me the serenity

To accept the things I cannot change

The courage to change the things I can;

And the wisdom to know the difference.

- Reinhold Niebuhr

ACKNOWLEDGMENTS

To my mommy
Freda Nieburg Gillis, MD (1914-2008)

And my daddy
Ivan Gillis (1912-1968)

How extraordinary you were.

The gifts were plentiful and directed my life

I am their daughter in so many ways.

My baby bro David Gillis and mein schves Renee Gillis
– Two of my best friends. We know each other.

Ivan, Sarah and Aram – made me an Aunt – one of the
most rewarding and defining roles of my life and from
them (with Eric, Sara J, and Rebecca) came Max and
Ezri, Jonah and Kyla, and Tova and Vida. The blessings
abound.

Brad Graves – my husband of 34 years – kept me eternally hip and helped me with everything and anything. A great love and a great life.

Roswell Rudd – full immersion life and love for 18 glorious years.

To Jennifer Maidman for our extraordinary collaborations and what she brings to it

To Tom Baschnagel who keeps it all going in top form.

To Michael Montella who kept it up and running

To Drebra Sterling and Paul Widerman whose help has been sustaining.

To friends, neighbors and community near and far

The heart is of infinite capacity.

Verna
The Older
In the middle of somewhere

Grieve In
Grieve Out

I was talking to a friend.

Told her that since the death of my beloved partner in 2017, what I miss most is the body body of it

You have to learn to hug yourself, she said.

I don't think so

I just have to learn to live with missing.

I went to the Coop

Could not remember the name of what I
wanted to buy

I described it to a man standing next to me

Green, flat, you put it in soup and it starts
with a P

Bay leaf he says

Exactly!

Jewsus was always trouble for the Jews

I often have no memory of yesterday.

I do however have proof it happened.

It is now today

and today always follows yesterday.

A good hair day for me is all about tweezing.

I spend an inordinate amount of time in my life in pursuit of miniscule hairs.

The gentle coaxing out, to the final extraction, elicit sighs of yearning and satisfaction

Sighs, which if heard from outside, would sound sexual

I worry about

Who will tweeze me when I no longer can?

For anyone kissing me it will feel like brushing up against a serrated fence.

We're all of a certain age.

I told him that no one had ever accused me of being cheery!

"I accuse you of being cheery," he responded

Thank you Ivan

I was recently asked to submit a recipe to a
cookbook being assembled locally.

Half an ounce of marijuana
Two bars of butter
A little bit of lite olive oil.
Sautee slowly.
Remove roughage
Let it settle.
Spread on toast.

It was rejected even though the person told
me it was the best recipe they received

They asked me to submit another one.

That's all I've got I told them.

Here today

Here tomorrow

I prefer that.

For now

Out of mind experiences –
rageaholics know about that

Truth is no stranger to friction

Everyone dies suddenly

She became a meaniac and our conversations began to feel as if we were playing ping pong with a grenade

Assholes always out themselves

I'm experiencing more synlapses

I got away with words!

Guide to Country Living – Part 1

What to do if you are in the pool and a bear comes out of the forest:

1 – You shit in the pool

2 – You get out of the pool

3 – If the bear doesn't eat you, run into the house

Hatreds and re treads

At long last I work and play well with others.

Most of the time.

I'd been reluctant to go anywhere much at all during Covid.

Didn't want to be exposed to the crazies, as I define it.

I made a rare stop at the post office to grab my mail from the PO box.
Masked and gloved. PO boxes right there.

Quick in and out

I get the mail, turn around and there's a man without a mask.

I look at him and say

To my mask....

Dumb motherfucker.

He looked uncertain as if he couldn't really believe what he thought he heard

I scared myself

I immediately turned around and left

The crazy person I didn't want to encounter

was myself.

Rageometer –to track your rage from
Zero to 10

1 - You take notice

2 - Your whole body chemistry changes

Emotional triggers start going off like
firecrackers.

And then you go through the roof of your
lost mind

We're all on a deadline without a specific date

That we know of!

The old demons retired and didn't even say
good bye!

New demons on parade here –

nightly in Kerhonkson

One aspect of relationships is that it keeps most of us from becoming homicidal.

You have a built in sparring partner

you get it on,

get it out

and then emerge into the greater world

seeming better than you really are.

How's your mental hellth?

No death is unexpected

Should I be worried?

I asked him where he was from

Idaho, he replied.

Oh, Idaho, Nebraska I said.

My husband did a sculpture in Nebraska.

One can't have less than nothing

People dis-pleaser was more my version

AA – Anxieties Anonymous

Do you come from a family?

Do you breath in and out?

Do you take in the state of things?

You automatically qualify for AA – Anxieties Anonymous

Every morning you will turn over to an anxieties sponsor a limited list of things to worry about that day

Only you can decide what that number will be.
To lower the number is the goal of recovery

If it is not on your list you cannot worry about it for today

If you have the need to make changes in your committed anxiety list, contact your sponsor

Why is what you committed to worrying about today suddenly not good enough?

The Case of the Shrinking Anesthesiologist

I went for my regular decade colonoscopy

I had a charming anesthesiologist from Azerbaijan

- I've always wanted to go to Azerbaijan I said

Why would anyone want to go to Azerbaijan he replied?

For the music and food of course I started to answer

Then I noticed he was shrinking

It was an odd sensation and confusing

Next thing I know I'm waking up from the anal probe

And understood that perhaps he hadn't been shrinking at all

My table had been moving up

To greet the eye level of the proctologist

Of course of course

Was he going to do this seated, bending forward?

Mystery solved

Family Gatherings = Regression Therapy

**The express track,
right back,**

**to all the unhealed
and sad places**

I was on the phone with a friend
and I suddenly realized
I had no idea what she was talking about.

I kept hoping she would say something that
would give me a clue
bring me back on board.

It wasn't happening.

I couldn't take it anymore and said

WHAT THE FUCK ARE YOU TALKING ABOUT?

Gratitude List for a really bad day

1. You're not a proctologist

2. You're not my dentist

Relationships are all about assisted living

It only took me 17 of the 34 years we were together to get it – he hadn't gotten everything he wanted either!

We both always had what we needed.

The days are getting longer
   The nights are getting longer

Go Gummys!

No one ever referred to me as his lovely wife.

I became the addict I lived with
And couldn't control

Unconditional love is a terrible idea

Whistling in the dark
Whistling in the light

You can never start over

Or begin again

You can however

Continue in a different way

When will the flat earthers come round?

He described his marriage as a 30 year
asthma attack

The next generation of addicts is upcoming

Marlon Brando Kissed Me

It was the end of an evening

Everyone getting ready to leave

*Marlon was doing the rounds saying good
bye, kissing goodbye*

*Then he kissed me – and our eyes sought out
each other in that startling moment of full
body recognition*

He knew. I knew. We both knew

The current of desire
Transpired
In both of us

Then I woke up.

It was a dream

I was 15 years old

That kiss has remained a visceral memory.

Few real life kisses came close.

What I've learned from playing poker:

The difference between a calculated risk and being an asshole

People saw me for who I was.

That was the problem

The pandemic showed me another level of alonelyness

Witness for the defenses
      Witness for the defenseless

Their relationship was proof of the theory of Unnatural Selection

Ideas are like clothing.

You try them on.

Most don't fit

You can't kill time

Simple Math – for a relationship

1 + 1 = 3

Can you see what you can't imagine?

A city friend rented a place in the country for
the summer

One night she heard a banging on the porch

Went downstairs, looked outside, and saw a
man in a fur coat throwing things around.

Of course it was a bear

Being from the city she could not imagine
being in such close proximity to a bear.

She was so brute-iful

My daymares far surpass my nightmares

Elicit drugs

Most were fuckers
Some became lovers

When one enters the Holocaust Museum

are some people sent to the right,

and others to the left?

Feeling less like myself would be such a relief.

I was extremely curtious

A Guide to Approaching Incontinence

The first big step is one of acceptance.

You no longer have any real control over your bladder.

Start wearing pads

You can order our brand FREE TO PEE YOU AND ME.

You will no longer have to worry about leaving stains on furniture or "going through" or even getting to a bathroom on time.

You can pee while you are standing around talking at a party.

No one will know.

Always assume you have to pee and you'll always be right.

Do not stop to wash dishes on your way to the bathroom. The water from the faucet will make you start peeing – if you haven't already

Do not send that one more text or email before going to pee.

Learn how to pee between open doors of a car anywhere at all

Most of all, you can now relax.

You have adjusted your expectations to the new reality

The Golden Years is all about peeing.

They got that right.

We all have to take a shift for ourselves

My emotions traveled at the speed of pain.

I need a nonaction plan

Fuck Siri!

One day my phone started talking to me.
I was startled and said
"what the fuck is going on"
My phone then said to me "that's not
very nice."

What?

I don't want my phone to have an opinion
about anything.

Someone programmed that algorithm.

Our minds were in sink with each other.

Even as a stranger I wasn't perfect.

The family is the pre-existing condition

Finder's Fee

I swim naked in the pool.

If I were to die in the pool whoever discovers
me will no doubt be traumatized.

Therefore I am establishing a Finder's Fee to
help pay for trauma therapy.

My mind is proof that dark matter is real

At this time of life

simply being alive

feels like enough

to have in common

with others.

VERNA GILLIS (1942 - 20??) has been performing "sit down comedy" standing up since 2010 when she won her first slam sponsored by TMI in Ulster County. The topic was Coming of Age which she changed to Coming of Aging. She was 68.

Her niche is aging - and so is she.

Her One Older-Woman Show is called *TALES FROM GERIASSIC PARK - On the Verge of Extinction*. She talks about childhood, the holocaust, addiction, aging, drugs, scones, peeing, and cancer.

United Solo Theater Festival, 2014 awarded *Tales* the **BEST COMEDIC SCRIPT.**

In 2019 she won the Woodstock Bookfest Story Slam.

She is the sole survivor of the band **THE OLDERS** which was with Roswell Rudd who died in 2017. Their video *AWESOME & GRUESOME - A Ranthem* is viewable at https://www.youtube.com/watch?v=sLInlX0FRAs&t=5s

Her three books *I JUST WANT TO BE INVITED - I Promise Not to Come (Life as One – Liners)*, *I'LL NEVER KNOW IF I WOULD HAVE GOTTEN THE SAME RESULTS IF I'D BEEN NICE*, and *THE I OF THE STORM* are available on Amazon.

Gillis has a Ph.D. in Ethnomusicology and taught at both Brooklyn College and Carnegie Mellon. She did field work recording music in Peru, Dominican Republic, Haiti, Iran, Afghanistan, Kashmir, Ghana and Cuba. Twenty-seven albums of these recordings are available on Smithsonian Folkways.

In 1979 she opened **SOUNDSCAPE**, the first multi cultural performance space and producing organization in NYC.

She was the first US presenter of African Pop in 1983 bringing King Sunny Ade from Nigeria which the *NY Times* called *"…the pop event of the decade."*

At different times she managed the careers of Youssou Ndour, Salif Keita, Yomo Toro, Carlinhos Brown, and Roswell Rudd.

Her most recent collaboration with musician/producer Jennifer Maidman can be seen here: https://www.youtube.com/watch?v=lOcay5PDzNY&list=RDlOcay5PDzNY&start_radio=1

https://www.youtube.com/watch?v=xKbZMHkSpWI

At 79 she's the oldest she's ever been.

www.vernagillis.com

Printed in the USA
CPSIA information can be obtained
at www.ICGtesting.com
LVHW091604090224
771439LV00036B/679